THE
LONG
FRIENDSHIP

BETWEEN
FRANK BIRD LINDERMAN
AND CHARLES MARION RUSSELL

BY
HAROLD G. MERRIAM

MOUNTAIN PRESS PUBLISHING COMPANY
MISSOULA, MONTANA
1979

Library of Congress Cataloging in Publication Data
Merriam, Harold Guy, 1883-
    The long friendship
    1. Russell, Charles Marion, 1864-1926 — Poetry.
2. Linderman, Frank Bird, 1868-1930, in fiction, drama,
poetry, etc. I. Title.
PS3525.E6392L66   811'.5'4   79-26310

To
and Frances
Alison and Alan

Acknowledgments

To the University of Nebraska Press for permission to use extracts from *Montana Adventure, The Recollections of Frank B. Linderman,* The University of Nebraska Press, copyright 1968 by the University of Nebraska Press.

To the University of Oklahoma Press for Permission to base the poem on *Recollections of Charley Russell,* by Frank B. Linderman, and to quote passages, copyright 1963 by the University of Oklahoma, composed and printed at Norman, Oklahoma, U.S.A.

To the Montana Institute of the Arts for financing the publication.

To Frances Logan Merriam for criticism and for yeoman work as typist.

INTRODUCTORY NOTE

The friendship between Frank Bird Linderman and Charles Marion Russell was warm and steady for nearly thirty years. They loved hunting trips in the autumn. Frank provided their meat with his rifle and Charley much of the fun by his good nature, his humor, his sense of beauty. When Frank built a house on Goose Bay, Flathead Lake in 1917 Charley loved to visit the Linderman family. He was fond of the three daughters, especially the middle one, Verne.

On and off the two corresponded by letters, Charley living in Great Falls. Frank saved about twenty of Charley's letters, dated from 1913, the last one written the year of Charley's death, 1926. They usually begin "Friend Frank" and end with "good wishes," and "your friend C. M. Russell." They are usually short and contain news about the Russell family.

The men complemented one another by nature and in their artistic work, Frank writing the tales, legends and myths of the Indians told to him by full blooded Indians, and Charley drawing, painting and sculpturing the life of the cowboys and the Indians east of the Continental Divide. Frank was nervous, quick of movement, ambitious and driving in his actions. Charley took life good naturedly as it came, was without ambition and devoted to his work.

PORTRAITS

I CHARLEY

Charley (Kid) Russell, night herder of cattle
Drifter in the closing life
Of east-of-the Continental Divide, early-range Montana
Toward the end of the nineteenth century.
Protege of Jake Hoover, old timer.
Habitue of the social meeting-ground of that day, the saloon,
Trading hasty paintings for whiskey — "Set 'em up barman.
My buddies, everybody,"
Generous, naive,
Happy-go-lucky, hail-fellow-well-met. In town
For a drinking spree and the girls of the Madame.
Today is today, tomorrow is tomorrow,
Life is fun.
Eight months living with the Indians, the Bloods, (Pikuni)
    in Canada.
"Horns that forked" to the Bloods,
"Running Antelope" to the Pikuni,
Sleeping Thunder, his friend, wished him
To wed Kee-oh-mee, beautiful daughter of a chief,
Charming, vivacious, fun-loving,
Wearing the snow-white elk skin garments of such,
Charley tempted, but broke loose and returned to Great Falls,
To the old life of herding, drinking, painting.
Never a thought of the worth of his pictures
So long as they traded for food and whiskey.
Yet always painting —
Accurate, getting better and better —
The scenes he knew so well — herds of cattle,
Bucking horses, cowboys on the range, in town,
Indians, more horses, always horses,
Spacious, brilliant country
Gorgeous, nature-gaudy.

Charley was rather of stocky build,
Not tall, not short.
Vigorous-featured of face, good forehead,
Straight, decisive, confident.
Long fingers covered with rings.
An impressive man of out-going nature.

II   NANCY

Nancy, a slip of a girl, a dozen or more years
Younger than Charley.
Uncultured, shrewd, conscious of pennies and dollars.
Good-looking, slender, attractive.
Love and marriage, she "Mame" to him,
He "Chas" to her.
Move from the tiny town of Cascade to Great Falls.
Break with the old life, but habits still strong,
Painting mornings, the saloon and buddies afternoons.
Mame holds up two fingers as he leaves home.
"Yeah, I know, two drinks," Chas nods.
("The damn woman is always in the way,"
Complained a buddy.)
In the bar of the old Park Hotel
A businessman from Boston. "I want you
To paint two pictures for me, so big —"
He measured the size by hands held apart.
Discovery that Charley's paintings
Had value as paintings — "You Chas, would sell
That painting for five dollars. My price is twenty."
Charley gasped, "It don't cost me nothing, Mame,
I just do it."
Mame from then on was the
Par excellence salesman of his paintings.

III   ARTIST

Before too long a time an exhibit in New York
("Frank, the lonesomest camp on earth, that big teepee.")

2

Then annual trips, annual price increases.
Friend of artists and actors — Fairbanks,
Irvin S. Cobb, Bill Hart, Will Rogers, others.
The big trip to England where his pictures sold
And whose countryside he loved.
In Paris — "Going to Rome? World's
Most wonderful art works there."
"Nope, not me, I'm goin' back to Montana and stay there
As long as I live."
Charley became famous as the painter of the old West.
Experimented and worked in sculpture; also casting
In bronze, and in writing — *Rawhide Tales.*
A man made, but still
The same unassuming, lovable person.
A career indeed.

IV   FRANK

Frank was of average height, lean,
Brisk of movement, well featured —
High forehead, straight nose, firm jaw.
Confident, but guarded,
Practical, efficient, ambitious,
Loving the free, outdoor life, the beauty of nature.
Longtime friend of Indians.
Charley was nineteen when he came
To the grasslands of eastern Montana. Frank
Was not yet seventeen, a child, really,
When he found himself alone in Flathead country
Somewhere near Bigfork,
With a leaking cabin, windowless, no fireplace, no chimney,
An animal skin for a door, and
An axe cut, deep on his foot, without food
Except for the deer meat he shot with an old Kentucky rifle.
That required a bit more endurance than he had bargained for —
"I felt mighty blue," he later wrote.
As a boy he had yearned for adventurous life
In a wilderness, studying a large map
To discover one.

V PARDNERS

He found that space in Montana in the eighties.
He met his first Indian, Red Horn, a Flathead warrior,
Who immediately spotted a pilgrim and befriended him.
For the next several years Frank was a trapper
Having been taught the setting of traps, how and where,
And the worth of different skins.
He had several pardners, all older than he —
Jack Bartlett, Black George (tough one, slave to whiskey),
Joe, Mike Therriault, Red Koonsaw (Indian).
Knows how to care for himself,
Seldom goes to town.

VI

The unspoiled country belonged, Frank soon felt,
To the Indians. Constantly in touch with them,
He became *Mex-shim-yo-peek-kinny*, Iron Tooth, to the Flatheads;
Later, *Co-skee-co-cot*, Man Who Sees Through Glasses, to the Crees;
Mah-phat-sa-not-tsas, to the Crows.
Sign Talker to them.
Frank met Minnie Johns in old De Mersville
And after many many months of heart-breaking struggles
To change his way of life, to desert
The freshness, the beauty, the freedom of the out-of-doors,
Married her.
(Charley five years later married Nancy.
About that time the two men met.)
Then began a scrambling life — mine keeper, assayer,
Prospector, newspaper editor, furniture dealer,
Finally insurance agent in Helena,
The spacious expanse of Montana his territory,
Money rolled in.
When he judged there was enough to live on
And educate his three daughters he
Built a roomy log house on Goose Bay on Flathead Lake
And began writing about Indians.
When a trapper and during work years he had made friends

4

With Indians, captivated by their simplicity, their naturalness,
Their love of fun, their humor, their
Customs, beliefs, their life in harmony with nature,
Their reverent spirit toward it.
He listened to their tales, legends, myths
Told by full-bloods, never halfbreeds,
Touched as they were, by American ways and ideas.
One day Opie Read, novelist, came to Helena, met Frank
Who poured out to his attentive ear the Indian materials
That enthralled him.
Three years later Read was in Glendive and again
He and Frank met — "Go ahead, print
The Indian lore," Read urged.
In 1915 Scribner's Sons printed Frank's first book,
Indian Why Stories: Sparks from War Eagle's Lodge Fire.
That firm published his next seven books,
Four about Indian lore, one sketches of a passing frontier,
One book of poems and one an excellent novel
Of buffalo days, *Lige Mounts, Free Trapper.*
They were topnotch folklore and history acknowledged
As such by folklorists and literary critics.
They should have brought Linderman fame
Similar to that brought Charley by his paintings.
But readers in the 1920s were not interested in Indians.
Linderman became discouraged, finally
Forced to recoup his finances.
Charley had illustrated the first three Linderman books
Then a temporary rupture entered their friendship.
Herb Stoops illustrated Frank's best Book, *American,*
The Life Story of a Great Indian, Plentycoups, Chief of the Crows,
Which brought favorable notice but not fame.

THE RUPTURE

"My father," wrote a Linderman daughter, "was something of a hero
    worshipper."
Charley was on a pedestal. He tumbled when, humanly,
He put off and off

The illustration of *Indian Old-Man Stories*
Until, of a sudden, Nancy, ever alert to sales,
Had a commission for $10,000 for Charley to paint
In the Prince of Wales Lodge in Canadian National Park.
Charley could not fulfill both commissions at once,
And that meant the loss of the Christmas trade for
The Linderman book, and Frank needed the money.
He was angered.
Nancy sent Charley to Goose Bay to tell Frank
He could not illustrate his book before the new year,
Once there the friendliness of the Linderman household,
In spite of Frank's anger, tied his tongue
And he returned home without delivering his message.
Nancy wrote Frank a cold short note.
He was enraged — "That means I must stop writing
And rebuild our finances."
The friendship cooled, though later Frank wrote,
"Charley was the most lovable man I ever met."

VII NANCY AND THE LINDERMANS

Nancy was never admitted into the affection
Of the Linderman family as Charley was.
Frank wrote: "My remembrance of our days
Together, alone in camp, and of
Frequent visits in our home on Goose Bay
Are highlights that heighten the passing years."
Not so Nancy. To them
She was possessive of Charley, her nature was not warm,
She was a social climber.
Infrequently she visited the Lindermans.
She had little interest in literature.
Her notes to Goose Bay were cold.
She was the hard-nosed bargainer for Charley's paintings.
The Lindermans seldom visited the Russell cabin
On Lake McDonald in Glacier Park, or
The Russell home in Great Falls,
Though Frank, whenever near, dropped in
For a visit with Charley in his tudio, "the shack."

INDIANS

Frank Bird Linderman from the time he was sixteen
Knew the Flatheads; later the Blackfeet,
The Crees, the Chippewas.
He was made a member of all three tribes.
He listened to their tales, fascinated,
Their myths and legends. And these
He stored in his mind
Ultimately recording seven volumes of them.
Why Stories, Indian Lodge-Fire Stories,
Indian Old Man Stories, How It Came About Stories,
American, The Life Story of
A Great Indian, Plenty Coups, Chief of the Crows and
Red Mother.
None of them his invention
Except *Kootenai Stories.*
Unlike Charley he had not galloped across the prairie with Indians
Or ever thought of living with them.
Yet, like Charley he understood them and their ways of life,
Enjoyed their humor, respected them and their lore,
Their cooperation with nature,
Their reverence for it.
"Well," he said to Charley, "guess we might be called
Friends of the Indians."
"Yeah," responded Charley," and of life in the West
Before she was spoiled."

II

"Russ," Frank said one day
Watching Charley's brush move skillfully
Over the canvas, "You never told me
How you came to live with the Bloods."
"Humph," Charley muttered, removing a small brush
He had been holding between his teeth,

"A whim. Phil Weinhard and Stilwell and me
Thought we'd like to see Canadian country.
We set out without too much grub
And we got there, but soon that grub run out —
My paintin's wasn't sellin' too well
Among the cowboys and Injuns —
So we rode over to High River Crossin',
Where there's a trading post, for food.
A lot of Bloods was there an'
I took a likin' to 'em.
I began makin' a bear in my pocket with some beeswax
An' a brave was watchin' my hand move so
I gave him the bear.
That was Sleepin' Thunder.
He was tickled to death.
Showed the bear to the crowd.
He wanted to say to me that he was pleased
But he didn't know my lingo, so
I used sign language an' he signed right back,
Sayin' why didn't I stay with 'em?
But when he proposed that to his friends
They weren't sold on the idea.
Just then Stilwell came with the grub
We needed for the return trip home.
"Nope," I says,
"I've just been invited to stay here —
An I guess I will,"
Sleepin' Thunder wasn't makin' progress
About my stayin' with his friends
Though they liked the bear, so
I took my pack off Gray Eagle's back
An' began to paint the crowd. Sleepin' Thunder
Craned his neck round
To see what I was doin',
Then two or three other Injuns looked, gruntin',
Then the whole crowd. That paintin' did it: so I was welcome
     among 'em."
Frank nodded, "So," he said,
"You spent a long time with them?"

8

"Six months," said Charley, "I liked
Their fun, the freedom of their life,
Their living with nature.
I learned their language, an'
Was named Ah-Wah-Cous, Horns that forked, Antelope.
You know I ain't a religious guy
But I bowed my head
When they worshipped the Great Spirit."
Frank said, "I, too, respected Indians
Though I've never lived any length of time with them.
Ever think of marrying a squaw
And living withm them?"
Charley had been still while Frank spoke,
His hands, heavily ringed, quiet.
"Well, there was Kee-Oh-Mee. She
Seemed willin' to be my squaw."
"Your pictures of her show you liked her," said Frank.
"They were painted with tenderness."
After a silence Charley nodded.
"So you came home."
Charley nodded again, picked up a brush
And put in a bold stroke.
"You an' me know Injuns an' like 'em,
We can even think with 'em, but
We wouldn't live with 'em —
You'd ferget you wasn't just an animal."
Later Charley was to write in a story,
"If you marry an Injun you've got to be an Injun, an'
A man ain't long fergettin' civilization,
Livin' with nature and her people.
He goes backward till he's a raw man
Without any flavorin'.
In grade, he's a notch or two above a wolf
Followin' the herds for his meat."

III   THE CREE SUN DANCE

The Cree Indians invited Frank to witness a Sun Dance.
They would set up for him, they said,

A buffalo skin tepee.
On his way to the dance he picked up Charley in Great Falls,
Knowing how delighted he would be to see
The lithe brown bodies of the Indians, swaying,
Flecked with firelight.
Their train was late but a small group of Indians
Was waiting for them.
After whoops and dancing, eager
To return to the Sun Dance,
They excused themselves and ran off down the road.
"Down the road, first turn left," they shouted back.
A tiresome halfbreed, however,
Clung to them, hoping, they surmised, for liquor.
The two men set off down the road followed by the breed.
"Two-tree mile," he warned them.
The air was thick and rain began to fall.
They caught the faint sound of beaten drums
And the high, weak wail of Indian voices.
"Long way," the breed again warned them.
"Ya can't get in dere; Cree let nobody see Sun Dance."
Frank and Charley ignored him, but he stayed with them.
"Little Bear, he de chief, a mean man
He no let ya in."
"Come along, Russ," said Frank.
With that the breed turned and walked back toward the depot.
"Long way off," he finally called.
Finally, they came to the village.
It was deserted save for dogs that barked
And snapped at their heels.
"By God,
We got rid of that breed," puffed Charley,
Chuckling.
In the blackness came flickers of firelight.
They pushed on toward the sound of the drums.
As they came to the Sun Dance Lodge
They heard a wrathful voice haranguing the Indians.
Frank recognized it and pulled Charley along.
"By God, I don't know about this buttin' in,"
Charley said.

As they stepped into the lodge the voice stopped;
With angry eyes the speaker turned
And sprang toward them.
He saw it was Frank and seized his hand, "Ho! Ho! Hi-eee"
He shouted, "Welcome," and led them to the
Center pole of the lodge.
"My friend, Charley Russell," Frank said.
Little Bear shook Charley's hand.
Then he reached for the center pole and took from it
An old otter skin, bedecked with eagle feathers,
Hawk bells and medicine bag and handed it to Frank.
"This belonged to my grandfather, my father and me,
All Chiefs of the Crees.
I give it to you.
Hold it fast.
It is big medicine."
Frank took the skin and fondled it, lovingly.
No more precious gift could an Indian make to a white man.
He felt like returning it, saying
"No, Little Bear, this is sacred to you," but
He also knew the pride of an Indian and that
The chief had made up his mind with suffering.
He could only express his appreciation.
Charley, too, was amazed.
The chief found good seats for them on the grass,
Cried, "Ho" to the drummers
And the dance was on again.
Charley said,
"Oh no, we can't get in there I guess!"
And got out his sketchbook.
"No . . . No, no sketches here. Just soak up what you see and
Sketch it in camp"
Charley soaked it in —
Brown bodies in rhythmic movement, supple,
Flecked with firelight.
The circle of drummers softly hummed
As they tapped their drums
With firelight flickering on their serious faces.
Outside of the lodge the dark, mysterious night

Was shimmering into wan daylight.
When the dance stopped it was early morning.
They bade goodbye to the drummers and dancers
And invited Little Bear to their lodge,
But he declined.
"Long time dance," he said.
Charley was silent as they walked to the lodge,
His mind full of beauty
Of what they had seen. "I wouldn't have missed seeing that
For a thousand dollars," he mused.
"It was great."
In the lodge he got out his sketchbook.

IV INSULT

"Did you ever have to swallow an insult, Russ?"
Charley was sketching by the campfire.
He nodded his head, "I reckon."
Frank said, "I was in Kootenai country when the Indians
Stole four of my horses.
The night before I came into Dayton
I had bedded down and was sleeping soundly, when
About midnight, I heard the thud of horses' feet.
I sat up to listen.
All I could see was the dim glow of my campfire-
The wind had kept alive.
I got up and groped toward dim figures
Dropping a few pitch shavings on the glowing coals.
I soon touched the mane of a horse.
Indians, you know, never roach their horses' manes,
And one of the horses had a roached mane.
Just then the shavings caught fire and
I looked at the head of the horse."
"Yeah?" said Russ encouragingly. "It was your hoss?"
"A squaw smiled from horseback on me.
It was my horse, Old Stub."
"What 'ud you do?"
"I got my Colt and ordered them off my horses."
"No fight?"

"Not in the face of a Colt six-shooter,
When they were gone I turned in again,
But I didn't sleep, fully expecting trouble.
About daylight my camp was surrounded by Kootenais.
They had torn down my barricade.
I got up and walked toward them
And received a slap across the mouth."
"Wow!" said Charley.
"Well," they were forty and I was one."
Charley chuckled
"'De chief,'" said a halfbreed,
'He say you gotta go way from here now,'
The chief was Aeneas, Big Knife
No one, you know, fooled with Big Knife."
"Umh," mumbled Charley.
"I said, 'You tell your chief I'm going on
Down to the Frenchman's at Dayton.
Tell him I'll wait there, till his people
Bring in two more of my horses they stole,"
"That's tellin' 'em," said Charley.
"When I get them I'll go up the country
Where I came from, you tell him."
The half breed spoke to Aeneas.
'De chief say you go odder way.'
"I saddled up, got the pack on the mule
And pulled out."
"Ya got your other two horses?"
"Yes, but the Indians followed me every step
To the foot of Angel Hill,
Singing and shouting insults because they had won a victory."
"Uhhu," Charley grunted.
"Well, what would you have done facing
Aeneas and forty Kootenais?"

CHARLEY'S UNUSUAL SKILLS

I CLAY MODELS

Charley always carried in his pocket,
Also in his war bag when on a trip, a mixture
Of beeswax and tallow for modeling clay figures.
Incredibly he would form a pig, a horse, a buffalo
In his pocket.
"A goat," exclaimed Verne, Frank's second daughter,
"You made it in your pocket without looking!"
Charley often molded animals in a pocket or under a hat
Especially for children.
"His restless fingers" wrote Frank, "worked marvelously.
I've seen him while talking and laughing
Cover a piece of wax and his hand with his hat
And without glancing at his work produce a bear, a deer,
    a pig, a dog."

Frank saw him one day in his studio
After several unsuccessful strokes,
Impatiently put down his brush,
Take beeswax from his pocket and mold a buffalo,
Set the model close beside him, picked up his brush
And got the effect he had wanted that his brush had not produced.
"Russ," Frank said, "did you ever use a living model?"
Is was a foolish question for always
Movement was in a Russell picture.
Charley looked at him amusedly and his belly
Shook with laughter,
"A human model would have a hell of a time
Posin' for me," he said.
"I'd have to spike him to a wall."
In a moment he added, "I get along all right
With mud."

II MISERABLE BUFFALO

"Had to fight hell out that damned bull," Charley said to Frank
When he had finished painting a large picture
Frank had persuaded the Montana Club to commission.
An immense herd of buffalo was crossing
The Missouri River, led by the huge bull.
"I believe," wrote Frank, "that fifty bulls
Must at one time or another have led that herd."
When the picture was examined by club members
A prominent one grunted, "Humph! That's a
Miserable bull in the foreground."
That member had warned Frank to tell Charley
To picture animals without movement,
Charley's effort to no avail, to paint a bull
Standing still, accounted for Frank's fifty versions.
In the end the whole herd was charging furiously.
Frank reported the member's judgment.
Charley, flushed with anger, stood still,
Took off his hat and scratched his head,
Cleared his throat, "Miserable bull, eh?
Well, mebbe he is a bum bull, but
He's the best bull I ever painted
Just the same."

III THE ENGRAVING

Charley was stroking the barrel of Frank's rifle,
"You roar like a cannon," he said contemplatively,
"And I bet ya kick like a mule."
Frank knew, for he was the meat getter on their trips.
(Charley, after settling in Great Falls had never
Killed a wild animal, though he loved
The meat Frank's gun got.)
"Mind if I cut some fresh meat on the old gal?"
"Sure," Frank said eagerly, "scratch her as much as you like."
Charley opened the small blade of his jacknife,
And began scratching the barrel.
Frank sat close, watching

In the dim light of the tent's lone candle.
The steel of the knife cut deep and surely.
An hour later "the fresh meat" was there on the barrel —
A buffalo bull, a buffalo cow and calf, a bull elk
A mountain sheep and a grizzly bear.
"Thar she is," said Charley, "An'
CMR 1913 is on her." He handed the rifle to Frank.
"Bully," said Frank, "She'll be with me as long as I live,"
(I have seen that gun. The cuts were so sharp
A print might be made of them.)
"Say, it ain't your gun," Charley suddenly remembered.
"No . . . no," said Frank ruefully, "It's Sam Hauser's, but" —
And Frank's eyes beamed, "I borrowed that rifle years ago.
Sam must have forgotten about it."
He looked lovingly at the engraving.
Some weeks later Sam's son Tom asked Frank,
"Have you father's rifle?" "Yes," Frank acknowledged,
And quickly added, "It would be too heavy for you,
And besides, it kicks like a mule."
He saw that Tom was impressed. "You go to Holter's hardware store
And choose the gun you like
And I'll pay for it."
That suited Tom. He didn't know about the engraving on the barrel
And Frank didn't tell him.
"Uhhu," said Charley, "and I'll bet
You've felt guilty all the rest of your life.
Ya know, Frank, I cheated a man once.
He was buying two of my pictures and asked the price.
'Fifty dollars,' I said.
Mean'n fifty dollars for the two of 'em.
But he counted out from his roll a hundred dollars
'An' I took it an' said nothin' 'cept 'Thank you'".
Charley shook his head.

AT GOOSE BAY — FUN WITH CHARLEY

On Flathead Lake no spot
Is more beautiful than Goose Bay.
There in the fall of 1917 Frank built a large house of larch logs
Well up from the shore line among evergreens and mountain
    bushes.
The curve of the bay ran
To the south to a massive outthrust of rock, a cliff, really;
To the west the mountains rose protectingly;
To the north a low-lying stretch of land;
To the east miles of blue water
Halted by the sharply rising Mission Mountains.

Charley loved to be with the Lindermans —
"He visited Goose Bay," wrote Norma, the youngest daughter,
"From 1917 to the fall of 1925."
The beauty of the physical setting, the close friendship
With Frank, the high spirits of the girls
Released tension. "He was always," Norma continued,
"Just part of the family,
Doing as he pleased — painting, reading, or
Falling asleep in the livingroom,
Snoring like a herd of horses on stampede."

II

He was with them as they moved in
Before the house was finished.
Mountain rats and mice came through
The as yet unsealed cracks between the logs:
"I don't mind 'em bein' chummy," Charley announced, "but
I don't like 'em sleeping with me."
One afternoon when he was napping, the girls and Frank
Were trying to corner a rat:
"There he is by the barrel," screamed one of the girls

17

And bang went Frank's gun, "Got him."
Charley's straw-colored hair appeared from his blanketed bedroom.
"What's going on? Camp attacked by Injuns?"
When he saw the dead rat, he slipped between blankets and
Assuming a Napoleonic stance, foot on the rat,
Proclaimed, "Got him."
He loved to play the buffon when at the Bay, and
Wherever he was there was fun.

Through the uncaulked cracks came also strong winds,
The kitchen range and the crackling fire in the large fireplace
The only sources of heat.
When Charley met anyone he would
Fold his arms, shrug his shoulders,
And shiver.
Bedrooms were made by tacking Hudson's Bay blankets
To the studding, color indicating one's sleeping place.
"Make mine purple," Charley said.

III

Charley enjoyed sleeping in the open.
When he visited in warm weather Frank
Pitched on the north projection of land His prized teepee,
      painted with thirty-six figures
By Mrs. Buffalo-Body and Mrs. Running-Deer, Blackfeet.
One figure was an old Indian chasing a horse,
A coiled rope ready for throwing.
Alas, the teepee was burned in the forest fire of 1919.
"Now," bewailed Charley, "You'll never get
A painted lodge like that one.
And the old warrior will never catch that hoss."

Candles glowed, blazes crackled in the fireplace.
Outside, the lake gurgled on the shore,
The wind softly huffed. Breathless from their dancing
Charley and Verne stopped to breathe.
"Oh, Charley, you are such fun," panted Verne.

When at Goose Bay Charley
Aped animals, dressing
In absurd costumes,
Dancing in his high-heeled boots,
Cutting up.
From fashion magazines he would exaggerate on his dolls
The already fullblown styles of dress —
"Got the last Vanity Fair, Verne?"
At times the long living room floor would be cleared.
Charley taking Verne or Norma in his arms
The two would dance down the floor, swinging,
Awkwardly bowing and scraping —
Anything to make fun.
He loved the fox trot, imitating in his face
The look of a fox, and in the handling of his body
The lithe and cautious moves of the animal.
On other evenings they played
Cards or Mah Jongg, Charley
Making fun of them, muttering
"Kung, Hung, chung, chung."
On such evenings an uncommon friendliness and intimacy
Existed in the Linderman home on Goose Bay.

Sleeping in the teepee.
Each morning he hobbled in his high-heeled cowboy boots
Over the rocky trail to the house,
Over the yellow larch needles, his breath on cold days
White in the air — "How! Hi-eeee! How's the
Swiss Family Robinson today?" he called.

IV

To bring supplies and guests to Goose Bay from Somers
About twelve miles up the Lake Frank built a sailboat
Twenty-feet overall with a beam of eight feet.
"She sails well," Frank boasted.
One afternoon as Frank and Charley arrived in the boat
Three excited girls were waiting. "Charley, Daddy,"
They shouted, "Hurry. Come see what's on Babe's bed"

19

A half-grown weasel growled at the men.
"Kinda likes it there. Let's catch him."
Charley held an apple box flat on the bed
And with a prod Frank urged the animal into it,
Scratching Charley's arm as it leaped away.
"Ain't he nervy, the dirty little murderer?" he said.
With much screeching of the girls and patience of the men
The weasel was in the box, a screen over its top.
At dinner that evening Charley queried, "What we goin' to do
With the little beast."
"Kill him," exclaimed the girls."
"Aw, let's feed him first."
Charley placed a dish of ice cream in the box.
The weasel licked the dish clean, then began to squirm,
Obviously ill. "He's sick as hell.
I'm goin' to kill him. Poor devil, he's awful sick."
He knocked the screen off the box and the animal
Leaped out and was gone.
"Ought to uv killed him," mused Charley.
"Yes," agreed Frank, "now he'll grow up
And kill less ferocious animals."
"God made him and rats and snakes and we
Wonder why," Charley murmered.

   V

For two years a squirrel made friends with the Lindermans.
They called him Tommy.
Each evening about nine o'clock they fed him bread and milk.
Tommy never missed the appointment.
For Charley the animal was a great joy.
His first words upon arrival at Goose Bay were often,
"How's Tommy?"
When he fed him he said,
"Ain't his tail pretty?"
The tail was sent to Charley when one evening
Tommy was found killed by a mountain cat.

VI

Walking slowly down the winding path from the highway
To the Linderman house, hat in hand,
Charley's face was alive with friendliness and anticipated pleasure.
The girls ran out, Frank following,
To greet him. "How! How! Hi-eeee," each shouted.
The path in early December, near the Christmas season,
Was deep in snow. It was the time Charley loved best,
He had a child's joy in the season.
He and the middle daughter, Verne,
The most artistic of the three, made
Gifts for friends, — little wooden dolls,
Models of animals, grotesque gnomes,
Fashioned of birch and shore wood
And painted vividly,
Or dolls dressed in autumn's gay leaves.
Frank wrote that they "raced around the moose maples,
The birches, the cottonwoods
Gathering doll clothes from their branches —
'Shopping at Birch and Company,' they said."
Evenings they huddled along the dining table, strewn
With leaves, pieces of wood, tubes of glue and paint.
They held up their creations for admiration,
"Wow," said Charley, exhibiting a just finished doll,
"Ain't she beautiful?" Of another
"She looks tough, like she's been eatin' hoss shoes.
My white women always look as tough as nails,
Like a hooker. Verne,
Let me see your doll."

Mrs. Linderman, small, quiet, sat in a rocking chair, reading,
Often looking up and smiling, amused
By their devoted fashioning of Christmas gifts,
Their jollity, their merriment.
Frank tended to the phonograph,
Looked over the shoulders of Verne and Charley, commented
On their handicraft, their ingenuity,
Wilda, the eldest daughter,

A bit straightlaced in what was proper and what
Is and is not art, was not quite sure
Whether a grown person
Should act as Charley was acting.
Norma, known in the household as Babe,
Bubbled with delight.

AT SANTA BARBARA

I FISHING

The Lindermans and the Russells in 1922 and 1923
Wintered at Santa Barbara
In neighboring cottages on the boulevard
So near the ocean that storms
Sent waves over their sidewalks.
One night a heavy storm blew up
And great breakers pounded the beach.
The next morning when Frank looked out at the water
He saw a boat driven ashore.
He called Charley and they examined it.
It was badly battered and stove in at the stern
And its seams needed caulking.
"Where we goin' to get some oakum?" asked Charley.
"Oh, at any ship chandler's," responded Frank lightly.
They shopped every such store in that seaport town
And, surprisingly, found no oakum.
Then, a day or two later when lunching with Ed Borein,
Western artist, their friend,
Ed with some amusement mentioned that the U.S. Battleship
     Oklahoma
Was anchored at Santa Barbara with a Montana lad an officer on her.
"Hosses must be gettin' scarce," Charley drawled,
"When Montana boys have to learn to ride battleships."
The two men, recognizing a source of oakum
Lost no time in looking up the Montana lad
And were invited for dinner aboard ship.
"Ask him straight out for oakum," urged Charley,
But Frank thought that would be brash.
All through dinner Charley kept nudging Frank
And whispering, "Ask him for oakum. Ask him for oakum."
Finally, after dinner Frank told the Montanan
Of their finding a boat on the beach that needed oakum.

The officer turned to a sailor
And told him to "get a bunch of oakum."
The sailor returned with enough to caulk a half-dozen boats.
"Wow," exclaimed Charley, "Sanford (a Montana taxidermist)
Can build us a buffalo with what we don't use."
The following morning there was no wind and the blue sea
Tolled lazily in smooth, dead swell.
They heavily caulked the seams of the boat
And left it to dry in the sun.
The next morning they pulled out to sea
Fully equipped with fishing gear.
Charley's luck was not so good.
He wasn't feeling well and lost interest,
Though his line was jerking.
"Pull in, Russ, pull in, you have fish on your line."
Frank called.
"Pull 'em in yourself," Charley growled.
He was draped over the boat's side
Sick as a dog
Frank pulled in Charley's line, and Charley
Squared himself on the boat's seat.
"Ever get seasick?" he mumbled. "If I was
A sailor and got seasick
I'd sure as hell get me a job in Glacier Park."
After that Frank fished alone.

AT A DINNER PARTY

The Lindermans and the Russells had been in Santa Barbara
        some time
When Frank asked a lady he knew well
To invite the Russells to a dinner,
Promising entertainment.
Charley arrived in a rented tuxedo, no vest,
Voyageur's sash and high-heeled boots.
Frank took a look and his face reddened.
The lady also took a look,
"What exquisite hands he has,"
She tactfully said to Frank.

All good story telling starts from a suggestion.
Neither Frank nor Charley could tell a story when asked
        directly for one.
After dinner the hostess said,
Quieting the table talk with her cultivated voice,
"Mr. Linderman, we have our West
Along the Pacific Ocean,
Tell us about your West,
The Rocky Mountains."
"I came to the Flathead country when I was sixteen,"
Responded Frank. "Mr. Russell came to the country
East of the mountains when not much older.
I was a trapper for many years
And at present I am writing the legends
Of the Plains Indians. Mr. Russell was a cowboy
And now he is a painter and sculptor
But both sides of the mountains
Have become spoiled for us — much too civilized.
Just the other day I was thinking of my life as a trapper —"
"With that scoundrel Black George," interrupted Charley.
He was off on a jag of story telling.
"Let us return to the drawing room,"
Interrupted the hostess.
Charley began with a tale not about Black George
But about Big George.
"As I was saying in the diningroom,"
Charley continued
"There were three of them on a hunting trip,
Big George, Dave and Old Becky.
Big George had just said that the buffalo he had shot
Was in a tree.
Old Becky grunted and turned to Dave
Who was turning a bannock in the frypan,
'Ever hear of a buffalo climbing a tree, Dave?'
'No-o-o-o, never did, but what the hell, Becky,
Ya can't tell what a young buffalo'll do
When he's after grapes.'"
This was heavy, outdoor humor but the dinner guests
Were convulsed with laughter.

Charley was into the next story.
It was about the same three men
Being chased to protection by a wounded buffalo.
Big George and Dave had shinnied up trees
But Old Becky hadn't had time to climb a tree,
He had ducked into a hole in a nearby cliff.
The buffalo had stood by the tree
Snorting and pawing the ground, but
Finally had wandered off.
Old Becky crawling out of his hole made a slight noise.
Quickly the buffalo turned and charged, tail up.
Old Becky, quickly but cautiously
Crept back into the hole.
Dave had been slipping down his tree
To get his gun, but he scrambled back up in a hurry.
At last the bull left, spent by his wound, and
Old Becky again crawled out of his hole.
"Ya damned fool," yelled Dave, "I coulda
Got my rifle and killed the bull
Ef you'd stayed put in your hole."
"Stay in that hole?" Old Becky shouted,
"Hell, there's a grizzly bear in that hole."
Charley followed with story after story

And the guests went on laughing and applauding,
Until Frank took Charley by the arm and,
Thanking their hostess, out the front door.

   III   THE SHOW

Santa Barbara hostesses often entertained
The Lindermans and the Russells,
Lionizing the two colorful story-tellers.
Charley and Frank were asked to put on a show
In the local theater
For the benefit of the Indian Defense Association.
They readily agreed.
Borrowing a tepee from Ed Borein
They pitched it on the stage, placing Norma,

The youngest Linderman, at its entrance.
In Indian costume the young girl,
Dark-haired, sparkling eyed, with a red streak
In the parting of her hair —
The way, Charley said, Indian women dressed for a special
        occasion —
There she sat with solemn countenance
Throughout the evening, an impassive Indian woman.
Frank told stories and legends about Indians, experiences
        with trappers
And poetic tales in the French-Canadian dialect,
With humor, yet seriously, in appreciation of
The qualities of Indians, trappers and Canucks.
He told of his pardner, Black George.
Slave to whiskey, gunfighter, killer of a man
With a butcher knife —
("I felt the knife go bump, bump, bump," he told Frank,
"Over every rib the feller had.")
"You know," said Frank to his audience,
"He never again while drinking whiskey carried a knife."
He continued, "One night we met where our traplines crossed.
A lynx was caught,
Ears back, mouth hissing, body seeming ready to leap.
Black George hit it a sharp blow on the skull,
'Big feller, ain't he,' he said.
Black George with a buckskin thong tied the near front paw
To the off hindpaw
Tucked his head through the loop,
Placing the body around his back and right side.
I followed, but didn't notice
That, in time, the jostling, upside down,
Was reviving the lynx.
Of a sudden George and the lynx were in a whirl of flying snow.
The lynx bit, spat, growled and clawed,
George swore strange oaths, striking out
Trying to get rid of the animal.
He looked at me shouting, 'Kill him, kill him!'
I did but I was laughing,
Not realizing the seriousness of George's wounds.

George, muttering, examined his clawed side, his arm, his breast.
Only his buckskin shirt had saved his life.
'Sorry I laughed, George,' I said.
We poured raw turpentine on the wounds,
The only medicine we packed, but George
Never once winced.
'S'll right, pardner. I must have looked funny
Fer a spell, I reckon.'
He began to laugh. We laughed together.
'Don't never fool with 'em. Kill 'em plumb dead
Before ya take 'em outta the trap.
Their cussed toenails raise more hell with a man
Than a sharp butcher knife!" George advised.
Through the audience went a perceptible wince
When Frank told of pouring turpentine on wounds.

Frank told Indian legends and ended by reciting his poem
"Pete Pebau's Lament."
      Me, Hi'm hol man — seventy tree;
      W're de woods was grow is prairie now,
      Hon de hol' game trail is work de plow,
      An' hon de plains dat uster be,
      By gar, de man is make de tree!
      De reevair, Ho! she's ronnin' wrong,
      Don' lak de reeple's hol' tam song;
      An' so we're de trout was jomp an' play
      De groun' is dry an' de stone is gray.
      Hi'm glad, you bat, Hi'm hol man, me,
      Hi'm please' Hi'm leave in tam por see
      De way de God is work de plan —
      Hi'm sorry she hadn't suit de man"

Charley, the more dramatic person,
Had a grand time, his voyaguer's sash swinging
As he moved about the stage,
Bringing western tales to life-
Whoppers, smart ones, sly ones, always
With a kick in the end line.
Some tales he told in the sign language, Frank interpreting.
This captured the audience's imagination completely —

How could one make an intelligent tale out of such indefinite hand
    movements?
The two men were at their best
Which was very good indeed, obviously enjoying themselves.
The audience, too, was having so much amusement that
On the following evening a second show was staged,
For a second packing house.
Here was something novel, something fresh,
Something unique, really.
The rich, high-toned proper society people forgot themselves
In amazement and enjoyment.

"That was a good idea, eh, Frank?" said Charley
As they walked to their lodgings in the late star-lit evening.
"And it made money for the Indians, too," said Frank.
"Shocked some of 'em, I bet," said Charley gleefully.

IV   HORSES

Charley and Frank were invited
By C.K.G. Billings, an eastern fancier
Who kept a stable of race horses in Santa Barbara,
To visit his stable—
It was large, airy and as neat as a pin.
The wide aisle between the two ranks of stalls
Was carpeted.
A horse tender led out to them
A black gelding, long-legged, with arched neck.
"A good-looking horse," Charley said.
And Frank chimed in, "Good saddle horse,"
"This is Uhlan," said Billings admiringly,
Reaching into his pocket for a lump of sugar.
Mr. Billings looked at them, puzzled.
He asked the horse tender to bring in another horse,
A sorrel mare. "Lou Dillon" he said proudly.
Charley accepted the lead, "That's a horse to take pride in,"
He said guardedly. Frank said, "Yes, she's a mare
I'd like to own myself."
Mr. Billings trotted her.

"Nice trot," said Charley. "Moves freely," said Frank.
Mr. Billings again looked puzzled and said something to the tender
Who brought out a small cayuse stallion,
The picture of grace and beauty.
"See the fire in him," said Charley.
"A beauty, all right," allowed Frank, "Has endurance, too."
"Great build," Charley added.
Mr. Billings looked discouraged. "Well," he said,
"Let's go up to the house,"
It was a palace with a gallery of paintings by
Corot, Monet, Innes — a score and more of modern painters.
Charley came to a painting by Rosa Bonheur, "By golley,
I can smell the cows that old gal painted,"
He cleared his throat, "She sure knew her cows and horses."
Again Mr. Billings looked puzzled.
"I want you to see my trophy room," he said.
There were scores of silver and gold cups,
Bowls and paintings of horses.
Mr. B pointed to a picture of a wild-looking mare,
"That's the mother of Lou Dillon. I used Pinkerton
To find that picture, but one day I found it myself
In a Montana saloon."
He looked triumphant.
"Maybe you painted it," said Frank unded his breath.
"Could be," agreed Charley.
A friend who had been tagging along with them said,
"Actually European royalty has knelt before Uhlan and Lou Dillon,"
Something in his voice made the two visitors feel
They should be ashamed of themselves. But why?
"Uhlan," he continued, "was the world champion
For nine successive years,
And Lou Dillon was the world's first two-minute trotter."
Frank and Charley looked at one another,
Wishing they could slink away unobtrusively . . .
"Yes, yes," they said. "Of course." They had admired
The cayuse stallion.
On their way home Charley chuckled,
"Just the same, that's a dandy little hoss,
That cayuse stud."

THE TRIP ON THE MISSOURI RIVER

One mid-summer day
When he sat in the studio watching Charley paint
Frank queried, "Say, what about that trip
Along the Missouri badlands?"
Charley whirled around, his brush in midair,
"Yeah, yeah, good idea, let's go."
He was astir with interest, "We been talkin' 'bout it
For two, three years. Sure, let's go."
"All right," said Frank. "I'll get a boat
Built in Fort Benton and we'll outfit her there
And put her in the water there."
Charley nodded his head and turned to his painting.
"Who's goin?" he asked.
"My father — he's visiting me —
And someone who can handle an outboard motor,
And you and me."
"You mebbe thinkin' 'bout Doc Nash?"
"Why not? He owns a motor."
"An' he's a good sport," Charley added.
Both men thought for a moment and Charley said,
"She'll be a big boat.
Four of us an' grub for a couple weeks
An' a tent an' tarps
An' beddin' an' all."
"Surely will," agreed Frank. "We'll make her big."
Charley stopped painting and said, dreamily,
"'Cept when we see somethin' interestin,'
We'll float with the tide by day
An' camp at night on a good beach."
He was full of enthusiasm.

One soft September day
The four men boarded the craft at Fort Benton
And pushed out onto the slow, deep water.
Doc Nash started the motor and they were off.

For three or four hours, all went happily;
The boat moved steadily on the quiet water.
Then, of a sudden, the motor sputtered and died.
(Outboard motors were new and temperamental.)
While Doc worked on it the three men paddled.
Suddenly, to his surprise and satisfaction, it spun merrily.
The men stowed their paddles and sang.
Late that afternoon they came to a warm, deep, sandy beach,
Landed, secured the boat, unloaded and pitched the tent.
Doc unscrewed the motor and lugged it
To a tarp he had spread and began removing parts,
Placing them in order beside him.
Frank and Charley were running here and there,
Whooping, yippeeing, exploring —
Boy-men ecstatic on an outing.
Father Linderman stood watching them,
Then, in derision,
Threw his hat in the air and shouted "Yippee"
In a cracked voice and danced a step or two.
The two men saw him, laughed and shouted, "You win,"
And began readying the camp for the night.

Off and on for the next three days
Doc tinkered with the unruly motor, adrift or ashore.
Finally, exasperated, and his ingenuity used up
He exclaimed with finality, "I'm done, I can think of
Nothing more to do with the thing."
"Why not pitch her overboard?" Charley suggested.
"It's makin' our food taste, an'
Stinkin' up our beddin'."
"Can't," snarled Doc, "this damn thing belongs
To Ralph De Camp. I borrowed it. Mine was out of repair."
Nobody said anything for a long time, then Charley burst out,
"A man's gotta be an electrician, a plumber and a master mechanic
To get anythin' outta that thing but a stink, an',"
He fumed, "He'd better be a preacher, too, or he'd
Go to hell when he died."
"Stow her under the deck," said Frank.
They did that and took to paddles.
The Badlands were wonderful, fantastic and grotesque,

Beautiful —

Carved in all shapes by water, frost and wind,
Crumbling and sliding, the harder parts resisting —
Stools, tables, spires, battleships, castles,
All that the imagination could ask for,
In constantly varying colors —
Rosy in the morning,
Glowing at noontime, with enchanting shadows
Deepening into purple in the evening —
The grotesque, the beautiful side by side
All massed together as if teaching, wrote Frank,
Appreciation by contrast.

One afternoon, beached and the four of them scattered,
Each intent on his own interest,
Frank, at some distance, saw Charley stumble, fall
And disappear. He hurried toward him. "Hurt yourself?"
Charley was scrambling to his feet on the rim
Of a deep hole, "Nope, that 'ud be a dirty trick on the Badlands."
He looked up amusedly at Frank.
"Say, that's a deep hole."
He dropped a rock into it
And listened for the strike at the bottom;
Sound came rumbling hollowly up. Grinning, Charley said,
"Why not drop the stinker into this hole?
I'd like to hear her go 'plunk.'"
"It would make a strike, all right," said Frank.
For several days Charley limped with a sore leg.
After the four men had stored their gear, boarded the boat

And pushed out onto the river
A swift current immediately took hold and crashed it against a rock.
There was a ripping noise and the boat began to fill with water.
The men paddled toward shore, jumped into the waist-deep water
And pushed the craft high onto shore.
They unloaded and spread the soaked
Food, tent, bedding and all

To dry in the sun.
They examined the boat — a plank
Had been torn loose from the transom.
They turned the boat bottom up and found two opened seams.
They stood looking at the damage.
No one felt like saying anything.
Doc picked up the plank and examined it,
"By gosh, she's been built with nails instead of screws."
That surely was bad news.
They set Father Linderman at work pounding out nails
With an axe, the only tool they had.
"Pitch," somebody suddenly said, "we need pitch
To caulk those seams."
They looked about them, but only cottonwoods
Grew on or near the beach.
"Handkerchiefs," said Frank and collected their bandanas.
He pounded them into the seams with a tool
Made of serviceberry wood.
"Charley," he asked suddenly, "Got any of that beeswax
In your pocket?" "Yeah," producing a small ball.
"Got any more?" "Yeah, some in my war bag."
Using all he had, still not enough.
"We can cut the pockets
Out of our coats," suggested the older Linderman.
"Yeah, and the tails off our shirts," added Charley.
After pounding in all of the rags,
"That will have to do," said Frank
"But we could use more."
Charley remembered his wet pillow
Which he had placed near the campfire
And snatched it away. Frank cut a rip in the casing
And pulled out a handful of sorry cotton.
"Just the thing," he gloated and rammed it
Into a seam. "That will have to do
Flood or sun,"
They set the boat on its side for quicker drying.
By sundown the blankets were dry,
But Charley's pillow was still soaking wet.

They had eaten their dinner
And were sitting inside the tent
Under a lowering sky telling stories.
"Equinoctial comin'?" queried Charley.
As he looked toward the west
The rain fell and through the night steadied.
The morning was clear and fresh and
They launched the boat
Early in the invigorating air.
By noon rain in earnest.
They hastily steered toward a wide beach to camp.
It was muddy gumbo.
They laid a tarp on the sodden ground and pitched the tent.
Nearby was a half-sunken abandoned old steamboat.
They loosened some planks and piled them
As a backlog for their fire.
Then the search for dry wood began.
With the axe they cut large chunks
From the steamboat.
That done, and dinner started
They sat disgruntled in the tent their
Feet to the fire, scraping mud off their boots.
For three miserable days they huddled
On that miserable beach while the rain poured down.
On the last day Doc, grumbling
Quoted something from Bob Ingersoll, sending Charley
Off on a tirade. "That dirty infidel never said
A word worth remembering for ten seconds." He went on
Muttering to himself.
"We need meat," Doc said. Frank picked up his rifle
And strode off over the gumbo
In the heavy rain. "I'll be back with a deer," he called back.
"Good," said Charley, who loved venison. He was taken up with the
Thought of hot meat.
A flock of birds rose
And he shouted, "There, Dad, there, shoot."
Father Linderman, quick on the trigger,
Brought down two birds — a ruddy and a mud hen.
Charley rushed over the mud and got them.

As he pulled feathers he commented, "Never saw a duck
That had feet like this one." They were balls of mud.
"It's a duck, though," said Doc,
Charley was satirical, "Dad, see if you can shoot
A hoot owl to flavor the stew."
The birds in the pot, they sat looking into the fire.
The tiny flames from the smoldering wood
Were green and blue and purple
And the ashes red brick in color. "A ghost dance
Of the river days," mused Charley,
"If I painted them just as they are
I'd be run outta town.
What makes 'em so pretty?"
Dad explained that shipbuilders often soaked their timber
In salt water and perhaps
The makers of the abandoned steamboat had done so, too.
"Time and salt and gumbo can do a hell of a lot of things,"
Charley said.
As they began eating the stew, Frank came in
Wet to the skin,
Dragging what looked like a mass of mud.
"Boy," said Dad drily, "why bring more gumbo into camp?"
Dad, as eager as the others for meat,
Was bustling about for firewood. "That old man," said Charley,
"Is good leather, good's any of us, an'
He's a damn good pardner. You know
Somebody's said that if he'd had God's job
He'd a made men grow young 'stead of old, an'
He'd a made health catching, 'stead of sickness."
"Are you in on all that?" asked Frank.
"Sure am."
"Do you know who said it?"
"No, who?"
"Bob Ingersoll."
The look on Charley's face made Frank sorry
He had trapped him.

The next morning the sun rose gloriously and the fresh air
Sparkled.
They lost no time loading the boat and setting off.

36

They had come upon a peerless day.
As they ran before a gentle breeze on the river
That evening, as they were falling asleep in deep content
The badlands spread out before them in splendor.
Rain fell again, turning to snow.
A coyote yelped. "There's your old friend, Russ," said Doc.
"Yeah, I heard him. He wants to borrow my slicker."
He sniffed, "Say, Doc, is your breachcloth afire?"
"Go to sleep, nothing could burn here."
Near midnight Dad and Frank were roused by Charley
Shouting, "What the hell's going on?"
Doc was shielding the blaze of a match in his cupped hands.
"Something *is* afire in this tent."

Charley began chuckling, "What you laughing at,"
Growled Doc irritably.
"Laughing at a man that wants a light
To find fire in the dark."
They all laughed and turned over for more sleep.
Snow blew into the tent and the raw wind
Was bellying the heavy canvas.
"Hey, wake up, Russ, it's your pillow burning."
Russ sat up, smalled, pulled at the pillow,
I'll fix her," he said, "good and plenty."
He rose, got water and poured it over the wisp of smoke.
For twenty hours the shoddy cotton had been smoldering.
Two days later the smoldering persisted.
Charley threw his pillow into the river.
"By god," he said, "if our granddads had had that thing
They could've had fire all their lives
Without borrowing coals from the neighbors."
"You should have saved the stuffing," accused Frank.
"Yeah should've," but he was not repentent.
The next morning was disgusting — snow and gumbo everywhere,
"Equinoctial, sure 'nough," Charley said.
Two more days they huddled in that miserable place,
While the storm raged.
Everybody was non-communicative,
Sullen, cross-grained.

The next morning Frank was up early,
Built the fire and shouted, "Yippee, the sun's going to shine;
We'll have breakfast and get out of this
Godawful, miserable place."
They were afloat by eight o'clock
Paddling in the foaming water.
Frank had rigged a sail out of a tarp.
The boat rushed with the wind through the water.
Overnight the weather had grown so warm
They had to jerk the venison to preserve it.

As they passed along the badlands
Observing the odd shapes, the colors,
The shadows, Charley read from the Lewis and Clark Journals
He had tucked into his warbag.
Once the boat stuck on a bar.
Charley leaped into the water to push it off.
"Them old boys," he growled "could go up this river with a load
An' we can't go *down* without gettin' stuck forty times a day."

As they near the end of their vacation
They had several warm, sunny days on the river.
With Frank's rigged sail
The gentle breezes drifted them along happily.
The motor, taken from under the deck,
Behaved and misbehaved, sputtered and choked.

Too soon they came to the end of their trip.
They beached the boat, unloaded gear and the "stinker."

All in all, the good days had outnumbered
The bad days.
They were content.

THE LAST HUNTING TRIP

Frank and Charley were walking down the deeply leaved and
   needled path
From the stage stop to the Linderman home.
"Wow, she's plated with gold." Charley stirred the yellow
   tamarack leaves
With his long, many-ringed fingers.
A deer trail crossed the path. "Makin' straight for the lake.
Makes you wish you'd been an Injun a hundred years ago.
Say, Frank, I got an idea — Let's stock up with
Grub and a lot of salt
An' strike out west from your back door
Till we kill a deer and then let's eat him
Right where he falls."
"Good, we'll eat a bite now, make up our packs
And light out."
The cold November day was perfect — the blue sky like crystal,
The sun warm.
The two men tramped and tramped
Often looking back to the indigo lake
Shimmering in the late sunlight.
At the top of a steep hill they stopped for breath.
"I ain't much good any more, my hind legs don't track
An' my tom-tom goes liketysplit."
"If you'd shed those cork-heeled boots you'd be better off
In country like this."
Frank had told him that a hundred times or more
But Charley's boots and voyageur's sash
Were as much a part of him as his face or hands.
Suddenly in direct line of fire was a yearling white-tailed buck.
"Shoot him quick! There's no meat as good in the world."
Frank shot him.
"He's plenty big enough, I guess," said Charley.
He had his pad out and was sketching the deer.
He never failed on any of their trips

To sketch bodies, legs, eyes, ears
Of any animal Frank shot.
"Fat, ain't he? He'll make good eatin'".
"Yes, but we can't eat him here, no water."
"How far to water?"
Frank took quick bearings, "About a mile and a half."
Charley took a few steps and groaned.
"My feet are blistered and mah legs are stiff.
I wish I was a crow."

Frank skinned out a ham
And they legged it through the twilight
To water, striking a creek.
They set up the tent, broke twigs and started a fire.
It was cold, very cold.
"Will there be a moon?" Charley asked,
His breath white.
"You bet, and a big one."
The wood would not burn well.
The meat would not cook well.
In the tiny blaze they fanned into life.
They ate half-cooked venison and, disgruntled,
Bedded down early.

The moon came up as big as the sky.
The matted leaves and dead ferns
Sparkled with frost. Every fir needle and tiny twig
Stood out in the moonlight.
"By God," said Charley, "if sleepin' on a
Bed of diamonds counts any
Our life's royal both ways from the deuce."
He shivered and tucked the blankets about his shoulders.
"Damned if a buffalo gnat
Couldn't look bigger 'n a grizzly bear
Up on that tree top." After a moment,
"Wonder how so many colors can get
Into frost out of moonlight."
Frank said, "Yeah, they borrow from the campfire."
"Frank," Charley murmured, "We ought to take

The damned fire to bed with us."
He turned over and rolled
A cigaret with his numb hands.
Even with his cigaret comforting him
He couldn't lie still.
"Why don't you lie still?" Frank complained.
"*I* lie still? It's *you* doin' the fidgeting.
I'd as soon sleep with a live bobcat as with you.
Here we are wrapped in two twelve-pound, four-point
Hudson's Bay blankets
And we can't sleep warm on dry ground."
"If each of us," countered Frank,
Had wrapped up in one of the blankets, as we should have done.
We might be warm."
Charley was silent for a long while, "Hell, pardner,
That ain't what's wrong with us . . .
We're gettin' old.
We ain't worth a tinker's dam any more.
It ain't the bed, the ground or the weather.
It's us. By God,
I'm going' back to your shack soon's it's light enough."
"What about this deer?" Frank asked.
"To hell with him. Let's pack him into your shack."
"Right." Then Charley burst out. "Look at that lance of moonlight
Dabbin' holes in that black water."
He was sitting up admiring fairyland.
"Wow, if a man painted that they'd call him a liar."
It was barely light when they had the camp
On their backs and were tramping to Frank's
Home on Flathead Lake.

The next year, 1926, Charley died.

The Long Friendship was designed and printed at Calliopea Press, Missoula, Montana. Linotype Garamond was set by the University of Montana Printing Department. Five hundred copies have been printed; of these, one hundred special copies are printed on Linweave, hand bound into wrappers and signed by the poet.